"*GOD* CREATED MAN IS
CREATED HIM; *MALE* AND *FEMALE HE* CREATED THEM.

Genesis 1:26

The True
Believer's
Marriage

Dr. C.M. Teague

Table of Contents

Preface

Chapter 1
Significance of Marriage
Your Marriage is Not That Important. Really?

Chapter 2
Opposites Attract
Not Really

Chapter 3
The Two Become One
In All Things, Really?

Chapter 4
The Dynamic Trio
Three is better than one or two

Chapter 5
Things to Do
Where Faith Meets Works

Dedication

I am so blessed to be able to worship and "do life" with the couples in a small group that I am a part of. I dedicate this book to the Hill family, Lombardi family, White family and Teague family. These families were willing to go through this book as a five week study in order to give me feedback and their experiences as they went through the study with me. We were able to take our time and make changes together; never taking our eye off the Word of God. I love and thank you all.

CHAPTER 1

Significance of Marriage
Your Marriage is Not __That__ Important.
Really?

Who is First?

You may not like this chapter and possibly decide not to read the remainder of this book after reading it. I will be honest and say that it was actually a continued challenge for me writing this chapter. It is a "doozy"! Well, at least it may cause you to rethink marriage and respond differently in your marriage. I truly pray that it does. I pray that it is the start of you having a marriage or single life, if you are not married, the way God intended. First, let me say that your spouse and your marriage do not come first and if you have children or ever have children, they definitely do not come first. Wow!...smack this guy in the head. No, please don't. That kind of sounds crazy, right? Well, over the years I have worked with couples before they were married and couples after they were married. In many cases, people seem to rely on their spouse or soon to be spouse for every part of their happiness or at least for most of their happiness. I have even seen people suggest that there is no one else other than their spouse who can meet their needs or they think they can meet every need that their spouse or soon to be spouse has. What pressure! What an unrealistic existence! We basically set each other up to fail when we operate from this perspective. Ultimately your spouse cannot meet every need that you have, nor can you meet every need that your spouse has or will have. So what do you do now? As believers we can benefit from being obedient to "The Greatest Commandment" that we find in Matthew 22: 34-40:

The Greatest Commandment

34 Hearing that Jesus had silenced the Sadducees, the Pharisees got together. 35 One of them, an expert in the law, tested him with this question: 36 "Teacher, which is the greatest commandment in the Law?"

37 Jesus replied: " 'Love the Lord your God with all your heart and with all your soul and with all your mind.' 38 This is the first and greatest commandment. 39 And the second is like it: 'Love your neighbor as yourself.' 40 All the Law and the Prophets hang on these two commandments."

The first and greatest commandment is not to love your wife or your husband but to love the Lord your God. Many people wonder why so many marriages end in divorce. I would argue that most, if not all, end in divorce because of disobedience to the first and greatest commandment. As you can see in this gospel of Matthew, Jesus definitely did not say that you should not love your spouse but there is definitely a hierarchy in the commandments of God's Law from which we benefit, especially in our marriages. Loving the Lord our God with all we have will make a big difference in how we see ourselves and our spouse.

Marriage Can Be a Distraction

Different surveys have been given to individuals, males and females, throughout the years in order to describe the percentage of people who desire to be married someday. The percentage of individuals who desire to be married someday was consistently in the high 90th percentile. Therefore most people in our society desire to get married someday. Actually, singleness is somewhat frowned upon. What would you say to or about a man or woman who is 35 to 40 years of age and never married? Some would say that this person is weird or has something else wrong with them…maybe commitment issues or some other issues with relationships. Nevertheless, it is easier to find a married adult in middle to late adulthood than it is to find adults at this age range who are single. This is a cultural phenomenon and perspective, not a spiritual, scriptural one. What matters as Christ-followers is that we keep our eye on God's perspective as oppose to the perspective of culture. Therefore, if a person decides to remain single for Christ for their entire life, that is a more than wonderful decision.

In our society, if and when we get married, we will more than likely find ourselves splitting our service time between our Lord and Savior and our spouse. We can safely say it is the nature of marriage. We have to really consider this fact before we get married. If you are already married, you have to be aware of this highly potential dynamic in order to make sure that we are not forsaking our first love, The Lord our God. Paul explains it best in I Corinthians 7: 32-35:

[32] I would like you to be free from concern. An unmarried man is concerned about the Lord's affairs—how he can please the Lord. [33] But a married man is concerned about the affairs of this world—how he can please his wife— [34] and his interests are divided. An unmarried woman or virgin is concerned about the Lord's affairs: Her aim is to be devoted to the Lord in both body and spirit. But a married woman is concerned about the affairs of this world—how she can please her husband. [35] I am saying this for your own good, not to restrict you, but that you may live in a right way in undivided devotion to the Lord.

Paul also says in his letter to the church in Corinth that marriage is not a sin. He says, "*[28] But if you do marry, you have not sinned ;...*"(I Corinthians 7:28). We can take some comfort in that. However, in that, we cannot lose sight of what will not only improve our marriages but ultimately improve our relationship with Christ.

The question is - "Is your marriage or will your marriage be a distraction to the first and greatest commandment? Prioritizing our relationship with God could definitely cause a sense of jealousy or confusion in a spouse who does not quite understand this commandment or an individual who may have an insecure anxious attachment style to their spouse or soon to be spouse. The first and greatest commandment can also be challenged when we decide to put the desires of others before what God desires for us, which He shares with us through His Word. This is something that I have seen in my own life and in the lives of others as they interact with their spouse, family members and friends. We can be so connected to the desires of humans that they drown out and over shadow the desires of God. This can definitely be a problem for us all. We can even see examples of this in biblical scripture when Adam, in the Garden of Eden, put the desires of his wife and his own desires before the desires of God and partook of the forbidden fruit. We see it when Sarah put the desires of her husband, Abraham, to have a son before the desires of God and offered her servant to her husband so he could lay with her and have a son. We see it when Abraham put the desires of Sarah to please him before the desires of God and he laid with the servant whom his wife offered to him. These decisions did not have pleasant outcomes for either individual. In those instances they allowed their marriages to become a distraction from the first and greatest commandment.

In today's world there can also be specific things within our marriages that lead us to put the desires of our spouse and our own desires before the desires of our Lord. These things can range from being distracted from having time to develop a relationship with Christ, to promoting worry, to the use of drugs, to the use pornography, to allowing others emotionally and sexually inside the marriage. I wonder how many times people have been distracted from praying, reading, studying or working for the Lord to do something that could have waited for their spouse or their children. In these seemingly little moments it would be wonderful if all of us could be aware of the importance of the first and greatest commandment and put ourselves second while supporting our spouses to put the Lord our God first. We should desire the same response from our spouse for ourselves so we can put the Lord our God first as well. As for the other specific human desires that I mentioned (and it is definitely not an exhaustive list), they are blatant sins and they also have to be completely eliminated from our marriages and our lives to have a true believer's marriage.

It may not make sense or fit with human wisdom but having a marriage that is a distraction to our relationship with our Lord and Savior is detrimental to our marriages while having a relationship with our Lord and Savior that is a distraction to our marriage is the ultimate benefit to our marriage. To have a spouse who is gaining wisdom about how to best live his or her life according to the teachings of the Creator, Jesus Christ, and the Holy Spirit is the best thing you can hope for when it comes to your marriage and your spouse's salvation. This is because these teachings are the absolute Truth on how to think and behave, not only in a healthy way but in a holy way. Please understand that as your spouse truly falls in love with God, He will become the most important part of their life. Jesus talked about this to the large crowds who traveled with Him. Jesus not only challenges us but gives us a warning and unchanging absolute truth about the cost of being His disciple in Luke 14:25-26. This gospel says:

The Cost of Being a Disciple

25 Large crowds were traveling with Jesus, and turning to them he said: 26 "If anyone comes to me and does not hate father and mother, wife and children, brothers and sisters—yes, even their own life—such a person cannot be my disciple.

Jesus also shares the importance of prioritizing our relationship with kingdom of God in "The Parable of the Great Banquet". He spoke of different life situations such as work, our possessions and even marriages in this parable. Jesus warns us that these things can be a distraction from the invitation to put the Kingdom of God first. He also warns us of the consequences of these distractions. This gospel is found in Luke 14:15-24 and says:

The Parable of the Great Banquet

[15] When one of those at the table with him heard this, he said to Jesus, "Blessed is the one who will eat at the feast in the kingdom of God."

[16] Jesus replied: "A certain man was preparing a great banquet and invited many guests. [17] At the time of the banquet he sent his servant to tell those who had been invited, 'Come, for everything is now ready.'

[18] "But they all alike began to make excuses. The first said, 'I have just bought a field, and I must go and see it. Please excuse me.'

[19] "Another said, 'I have just bought five yoke of oxen, and I'm on my way to try them out. Please excuse me.'

[20] "Still another said, 'I just got married, so I can't come.'

[21] "The servant came back and reported this to his master. Then the owner of the house became angry and ordered his servant, 'Go out quickly into the streets and alleys of the town and bring in the poor, the crippled, the blind and the lame.'

[22] "'Sir,' the servant said, 'what you ordered has been done, but there is still room.'

23 "Then the master told his servant, 'Go out to the roads and country lanes and compel them to come in, so that my house will be full. 24 I tell you, not one of those who were invited will get a taste of my banquet.'"

Putting Marriage in Its Place

As believers, we know that there is an after-life. That after-life will be eternal and joyful or eternal torment and death. I hope as true believers we already knew that fact. What does this have to do with marriage? Well, understanding the context in which marriage is important is beneficial for understanding marriage. In this life, as we all know, we can marry and be given in marriage. However, Jesus tells us the limitations of marriage as it relates to context. This limitation tells us the importance of marriage in life and the after-life. Jesus explains this limitation in His conversation with the Sadducees in Mark 12:18-27. This gospel says:

18 Then the Sadducees, who say there is no resurrection, came to him with a question. 19 "Teacher," they said, "Moses wrote for us that if a man's brother dies and leaves a wife but no children, the man must marry the widow and raise up offspring for his brother. 20 Now there were seven brothers. The first one married and died without leaving any children.21 The second one married the widow, but he also died, leaving no child. It was the same with the third. ²² In fact, none of the seven left any children. Last of all, the woman died too. ²³ At the resurrection whose wife will she be, since the seven were married to her?"

²⁴ Jesus replied, "Are you not in error because you do not know the Scriptures or the power of God? ²⁵ When the dead rise, they will neither marry nor be given in marriage; they will be like the angels in heaven. ²⁶ Now about the dead rising—have you not read in the Book of Moses, in the account of the burning bush, how God said to him, 'I am the God of Abraham, the God of Isaac, and the God of Jacob'? ²⁷ He is not the God of the dead, but of the living. You are badly mistaken!"

      Jesus lets us know in the scripture above that we will not marry or be given in marriage in the after-life, the new heavens and the new earth. I would imagine that if marriage was an eternally important state of existence then we would marry and be given in marriage in the new earth. The eternally important state of existence in the after-life, the new earth, is joyful worship and fellowship amongst the community of true believers. We are given this Truth in Isaiah, Revelations and other biblical scripture. Isaiah 66:22-24 tells us about the joyful worship that will take place when there are the new heavens and the new earth that God will create for those who are faithful. Isaiah was a prophet of God who spoke to the nations around him about salvation. The book is a collection of oracles, prophecies, and reports in the Old Testament. Isaiah 66:22-24 says:

[22] "As the new heavens and the new earth that I make will endure before me," declares the LORD, "so will your name and descendants endure. [23] From one New Moon to another and from one Sabbath to another, all mankind will come and bow down before me," says the LORD. [24] "And they will go out and look on the dead bodies of those who rebelled against me; the worms that eat them will not die, the fire that burns them will not be quenched, and they will be loathsome to all mankind."

Revelations 21:1-8 tells us about our joyful fellowship and the kind of existence that will take place in the new earth for those who are victorious. After you read the scripture from Revelations below, take some time to look at Isaiah 65:17-25 in order to see other scripture that shows us what the after-life experience will be like in the new heavens and new earth.

Revelations 21:1-8

[1] Then I saw "a new heaven and a new earth," for the first heaven and the first earth had passed away, and there was no longer any sea. [2] I saw the Holy City, the New Jerusalem, coming down out of heaven from God, prepared as a bride beautifully dressed for her

husband. ³ And I heard a loud voice from the throne saying, "Look! God's dwelling place is now among the people, and he will dwell with them. They will be his people, and God himself will be with them and be their God. ⁴ 'He will wipe every tear from their eyes. There will be no more death' or mourning or crying or pain, for the old order of things has passed away."

⁵ He who was seated on the throne said, "I am making everything new!" Then he said, "Write this down, for these words are trustworthy and true."

⁶ He said to me: "It is done. I am the Alpha and the Omega, the Beginning and the End. To the thirsty I will give water without cost from the spring of the water of life. ⁷ Those who are victorious will inherit all this, and I will be their God and they will be my children. ⁸ But the cowardly, the unbelieving, the vile, the murderers, the sexually immoral, those who practice magic arts, the idolaters and all liars—they will be consigned to the fiery lake of burning sulfur. This is the second death."

As we can see from various scriptures in the New and Old Testament, marriage can be a very important experience in our earthly lives as we strive to be Christ-like. However, in our "heavenly lives" it will not exist, but the most important relationship will still exist and that is our relationship with our Heavenly Father.

Do not get me wrong. It is not my intent to discourage marriage or to belittle it in any way. It is my intent to help us have the only perspective about marriage that matters and that is God's perspective. In I Corinthians 7:8-9, 36-38, Paul gives us wisdom related to when it is best for us to get married. It is not before we reach a certain age, nor is it once we have reached certain goals, as these reasons reflect human wisdom, wisdom that has been birthed in culture. I would argue that this is not wisdom at all compared to the divine wisdom that comes from God. Believe me, He knows better than we do. In I Corinthians 7;8-9, 36-38, Paul says:

8 Now to the unmarried and the widows I say: It is good for them to stay unmarried, as I do. 9 But if they cannot control themselves, they should marry, for it is better to marry than to burn with passion.

36 If anyone is worried that he might not be acting honorably toward the virgin he is engaged to, and if his passions are too strong and he feels he ought to marry, he should do as he wants. He is not sinning. They should get married. 37 But the man who has settled the matter in his own mind, who is under no compulsion but has control over his own will, and who has made up his mind not to marry the virgin— this man also does the right thing. 38 So then, he who marries the virgin does right, but he who does not marry her does better.

Wow!! So what do we do with that little nugget of wisdom? Well, if we are single, it sounds like we'd better start practicing some control over our own will and if we are married, well, at least we have done the second best thing. There is still hope for us all. However, are you starting to feel like some of the hope depends on you and what you do in your marriage? I believe that for those of us who are married, we now have to pray about being good multi-taskers. I want to emphasize prayer because our marriages *need* prayer, not only to be successful for the man and woman involved but ultimately that the marriage is successful at allowing Jesus Christ to be the biggest part of the marital experience. We have to take care of how we pray, worship, treat our spouse, and fellowship with others.

Marriage is a very important opportunity to display the love of Christ within a covenant between a man and a woman. It is the most important human to human relationship a man and woman can have. Our Savior Jesus Christ said, *"Haven't you read," he replied, "that at the beginning the Creator 'made them male and female,' and said, 'For this reason a man will leave his father and mother and be united to his wife, and the two will become one flesh'? So they are no longer two, but one flesh. Therefore what God has joined together, let no one separate."* (Matthew 19:4-6). As we can see, Jesus himself talked about the intimate and faithful nature of marriage between a man and a woman. He also desires an intimate and faithful relationship with each of us. If we are persistent at seeking that relationship with Christ, we then can truly share the love of Christ within our marriages. A man and a woman can then truly expect their marriage to mature towards a holy marriage as well as a happy and peaceful marriage. In the previous sentences I emphasize the words man and woman because in all of God's Word, when He talks about marriage, He never pairs man with anyone or anything else other than woman and He never pairs woman with anyone or anything else other than man. God's Word never pairs man with man or women with women or man with animals or woman with animals or man with earthly things or woman with earthly things without speaking out against such unions. You can look for yourself. You will see this truth throughout scripture. Therefore, anything outside of a marital covenant between a man and a woman is not a true believers marriage; it is not a holy marriage. This is very important to know because it is true and therefore foundational. When we think about putting marriage in its place we have to think about who we marry as well, which we will discuss in the next chapter.

Conclusion

Now we come to the conclusion of this chapter and we prepare to dig deeper as it relates to looking into our own marriages and our thoughts and behaviors related to putting Christ first, recognizing marital distractions, and putting marriage in its holy place. It is time to take marriage more seriously and this can be done by making it second in relation to the first and greatest commandment. It is time to take marriage more seriously and this can be done by being aware of the difference between a societal perspective and God's Truth about marriage. We must continuously ask ourselves what God would say about the condition of our marriage or what He would say about what we believe about marriage.

CHAPTER 1 - Digging Deeper

In this part of each chapter we will attempt to "dig deeper" by honestly considering specific questions related to what we just read in the chapter. Feel free to consider and discuss questions that you have that I did not include. This process must be taken seriously as it will hopefully shed light on areas in our marriage that need to be maintained, changed or established. Therefore, I want to start "Digging Deeper" and the remainder of the chapters with a prayer. You can use the prayer that I have said and written in each chapter or you can say your own. The important thing is to pray.

Our Prayer for this chapter

Dear and Gracious Heavenly Father, we approach your throne humbled and thankful. We thank you for this opportunity to continue to better our relationship with You regardless of the outcome of anything else in our lives. We pray that You soften our hearts and give us the courage to be obedient to Your will as it relate to marriage. We thank You for Your Holy Spirit and pray that He helps us guide our thoughts, responses and the words from our months as we consider and discuss these questions related to our relationship with You and our marriage. We have faith in Your love, Your mercy, Your righteousness, and Your Truth. In Jesus Christ's name we pray. AMEN!

Chapter 1 Questions
(*Extra Space for Responses on pages 86-87*)

1. What are your thoughts about putting God first in your marriage? How do you feel about your fiancé or spouse putting Christ first in their life?

2. What is something that you do in your life that shows you are interested in *loving the Lord your God with all your heart and with all your soul and with all your mind*? How much time do you spend doing this?

3. What is something that you want to start doing in your life that shows you are interested in *loving the Lord your God with all your heart and with all your soul and with all your mind*?

4. What are some specific distractions to your relationship with Christ in your life today?

5. In what ways has your relationship, marriage or family life presented as a distraction to your relationship with Christ?

6. In what ways have you presented as a distraction for your fiancé or spouse in their relationship with Christ?

7. In this chapter we discussed the context in which marriage is important. What are your thoughts about that? How could you start or increase your interaction with a community of believers?

CHAPTER 2

Opposites Attract
Not Really

Opposites Attract…One of the Biggest Lies Ever Told

We have always heard that opposites attract. This is true when we are talking about magnets. However, people are not magnets. This "opposites attract" notion can also be true when people have a lack of love for themselves due to not understanding or believing who they are through the love that God has given them and the love He has for them. If we are blind to our true identity in Christ it is difficult to be loyal to that identity, which may cause us to seek something opposite of ourselves. I would say that this is how the "opposites attract" expression has been able to be transferred from magnets to people. I have seen and heard of people living by this notion, starting relationships based on it and even getting married to their *opposite*. I have also seen the struggles that have come from couples trying to start and maintain a relationship using this notion. The truth is that *opposites* do not attract and do not attract well for long periods of time in marriage. Therefore, I find it safe to say that "opposites attract" is one of the biggest lies ever told. So, what do we do? Well, first, we do not start "dating relationships" and marriages with people who are our opposite and if we are already married to someone we feel is an *opposite*, we work honestly to change those things that make us *opposite* with the help of Christ.

Of course we know that most couples have different characteristics such as; he likes the color blue and she likes the color red, she really likes Mexican food (my wife) and he really likes pizza, grilled cheese, cold cereal, and cheeseburgers (that would be me), he may be an "introvert" and she may be an "extrovert" etc. A marriage can definitely survive these little differences, however too many differences will more than likely lead to low marital satisfaction. Low martial satisfaction can affect the holiness of our marriage and God knows this about us. What he really wants us to focus on is the biggest *opposite* challenge for couples. The biggest *opposite* challenge for couples is when the *opposites* are related to personal values such as; he is a believer and she is not, she believes church is important and he does not, she does not believe in having new friends of the *opposite* sex and he believes it is okay, she believes getting drunk or high is okay and he does not, she believes that the use of profanity is appropriate and he does not, he believes it is okay to have late nights and she does not, he believes that it is okay to watch pornography and she does not etc. These are definitely personal value differences. Value differences can also show up in how couples desire to raise children, which can be very troublesome as well. Researchers interested in understanding successful marriages have conducted studies and have come to find the importance of "homogamy". Homogamy is a marriage in which a man and a woman are similar to each other. These researchers could have actually saved themselves the trouble and simply look at biblical scripture to gain this Truth and understanding from God. Paul warns believers in I Corinthians 6:14-16 to not be yoked with someone who has different beliefs and values. Paul says:

[14] Do not be yoked together with unbelievers. For what do righteousness and wickedness have in common? Or what fellowship can light have with darkness? [15] What harmony is there between Christ and Belial? Or what does a believer have in common with an unbeliever? [16] What agreement is there between the temple of God and idols? For we are the temple of the living God. As God has said: "I will live with them and walk among them, and I will be their God, and they will be my people."

God's desires expressed through Paul's letter to the church in Corinth is more than beneficial to our lives in general and therefore is more than beneficial to us in our dating and marital relationships. It requires us to seek like-mindedness, not *opposites*, in our relationships. The ultimate goal is to search for, desire and work towards holiness in our dating and our marital relationship. That requires us to seek Christlikeness and to be honest with ourselves and others within our relationships, dating or marriage. The truth is, who really wants to date or marry a liar and who really wants to live as a liar in a dating relationship or marriage? This is what happens when we do not share our true selves to those we date and marry. We may end up with an *opposite*.

How did and how do you present yourself to your spouse or in your dating relationship? Is that self-presentation restricted or open? Sometimes in our interpersonal interactions we knowingly or unknowingly monitor our self-presentations and of course sometimes we do not. How do these opposite styles of self-monitoring affect the marital or dating relationship? Self-monitoring refers to how we modify or restrain expressions of emotion, verbiage, behavior, and other forms of self-presentation. Some people are high self-monitors and some people are low self-monitors. High self-monitors employ a premeditated self-presentation whereas low self-monitors employ a more genuine self-presentation. High self-monitors socialize in a more superficial way and their interpersonal relationships are not close, while low self-monitors socialize with a deeper connection. How does this transfer into the marital relationship? Similar to other social relationships, low self-monitors seem to be closer and more attached in their marriage and similar to other social relationships high self-monitors seem to be less attached in their marriages. Therefore, low self-monitors tend to have more genuine and constructive reactions to conflict. The best way for a man and a woman to learn the important personal things about each other is to avoid holding back their true self. If a "naked expression of the self" does not take place or comes too late (i.e. after relationship commitment) and we learn that our fiancé or spouse does not have the same beliefs and values that we have; we can become ashamed of that person or at least ashamed of the characteristic that is *opposite*. There needs to be a *naked expression of the self* from the beginning. If there is not a "good fit", it is better to know it now than to learn it later. When we find someone who has the same beliefs and values that we have, we feel blessed to have this person in our lives, not ashamed. In Genesis 2:23-25, Adam expresses his feelings of being blessed and lack of shame. It reads:

23 The man said, "This is now bone of my bones and flesh of my flesh; she shall be called 'woman,' for she was taken out of man."
24 That is why a man leaves his father and mother and is united to his wife, and they become one flesh.
25 Adam and his wife were both naked, and they felt no shame.

We can see from this scripture that Adam and Eve were very close, similar and really knew each other. They were not opposite of each other. If "*opposite*" was better, I believe God would have never made Eve bone of Adam's bone and flesh of Adam's flesh.

There is a dating relationship in scripture that gives us a good example of *opposites* turning into disaster. That relationship is the relationship between Samson and Delilah. Samson was blessed by God, often filled with the Spirit of the Lord and leader of the Israelites for twenty years during the days of the Philistines (Judges 13:24-25, Judges 15:20) and

Delilah was a woman from the Valley of Sorek who was not filled with the Spirit of the Lord. They were not equally yoked. Samson seemed to be blind to the fact that he was not equally yoked with Delilah. This allowed her to lie and deceive him, have secrets in her relationship with him and ultimately contribute to his death. Samson fell in love with the wrong women and ultimately he was influenced to put the desires of his girlfriend before the desires of God which was a product of Samson and Delilah being *opposites*. Samson was drawn to her beauty from the beginning and fell in love with her initial presentation. The things that initially draws us to our spouse or the person we are dating is never the whole truth but can definitely be the start of something good or something not so good.

The seemingly positive factors that initially draw a man and a woman together indicate potential marital choice, but not marital success. Positive expectations in a dating relationship do not necessarily equal a positive marriage. However, positive expectations can be beneficial because they can inspire healthy interactions between spouses that in turn lead to positive outcomes. It is also important to understand that positive expectations can be detrimental if too many *opposite* characteristics are present causing expectations to not be met and therefore causing relationship disappointment. When positive expectations are paired with positive relationship skills and even when negative expectations are paired with less positive relationship skills there is more stable dating and marital satisfaction over time because the expectations and skills are not opposite. When they are *opposite* we will see a steeper decline in dating and marital satisfaction. That is, if positive skills are paired with less positive expectation and if negative skills are paired with positive expectations there is a steeper decline in dating and marital satisfaction. I feel like I have said a lot in these few sentences but if you really think about these pairings playing out in "real life", you will be able to imagine the positive and negative outcomes. Basically, our marriages do better when our expectations and our skills are not *opposite.*

Truthfully our expectations and skills can be enhanced by our obedience to God and our heart's desire to live in harmony with our spouse. In Paul's letter to the church at Philippi, he encourages this type of response in our daily interactions. The Holy Spirit through Paul by way of our Savior encourages us to imitate the humility of Christ. Philippians 2:1-3 says:

[1] Therefore if you have any encouragement from being united with Christ, if any comfort from his love, if any common sharing in the Spirit, if any tenderness and compassion, [2] then make my joy complete by being like-minded, having the same love, being one in spirit and of one mind. [3] Do nothing out of selfish ambition or vain conceit. Rather, in humility value others above yourselves,

Peter's letter to early Christians was written to encourage them in their daily walk of faith and has some similarities to the message in Paul's letter to the church in Philippi mentioned above. 1 Peter 3:8 says:

8 Finally, all of you, be like-minded, be sympathetic, love one another, be compassionate and humble.

In a true believer's marriage we always want to consider our marriage over any selfish desire. This is a delicate dance between husband and wife that requires the synchronizing (i.e. harmonizing) of what God desires for our marriage and your spouse and your desires and expectations. I am smiling right now because hear is another situation in which God really shows us that His wisdom trumps our wisdom or lack of wisdom every single time. The thing is, when we focus on what God desires even if it is uncomfortable or seems like it is not going to work, in the end it works and even creates more peace in our marriage over time. We just have to trust God and be open with our spouse about our thoughts and feelings.

CHAPTER 2 - Digging Deeper

We are once again we back to the part the chapter in which we will attempt to "dig deeper" by honestly considering specific questions related to what we just read in the chapter. Feel free to consider and discuss questions that you have that I did not include. I have provided another prayer to consider prior to addressing these questions. You can use the prayer that I have said and written below or you can say your own. The important thing is to pray.

Our Prayer for this chapter

Dear heavenly Father, our merciful and righteous Creator. Once again we come humbled and willing to know Your Truth for our marriage. We thank You for this opportunity to be with You as we explore our opposite characteristics. We pray that You give us the wisdom to understand what does and does not need to change in our marriage and the courage to make changes according to that wisdom. We pray that You help us to watch over the words that come out of our mouths as we discuss questions related to this chapter. In Jesus Christ's name we pray, AMEN!

Chapter 2 Questions

(Extra Space for Responses on pages 88-89)

1. "Opposites attract", what has been your thoughts about this notion in the past? What are your thoughts about this notion now?

2. What are some personal characteristics and values of others that you find unattractive? Do you have any of these characteristics?

3. In your marriage or dating relationship, what are some similar personal characteristics between you two?

4. In your marriage or dating relationship, what are some opposite personal characteristics between you two?

5. Thinking about the opposite characteristics, which one(s) can you live with and why? In what ways have you attempted to keep these opposites from becoming a negative force in your marriage?

CHAPTER 3

The Two Become One
In All Things? Really?

One Plus One Equals One (1+1=1)

One plus one equals one is more likely to occur when we are equally yoked with our spouse. This equation is much harder to achieve if we are not, but with prayer, faith, work and dedication we can hopefully achieve this equation. We must become one and do things that promote this oneness if we desire a true believer's' marriage, a Godly marriage. So what does it actually mean to become "one"? Actually, I believe that there are many "moving parts" (areas) in the process to becoming "one" and as we discuss these areas you may actually disagree. The fact is, when our Lord and Savior says the" two" becomes "one", I believe He means for us to become "one" in all things, not just "one" in areas we are most comfortable. Different biblical scripture speak of this Godly oneness.

The 2 Become 1

Genesis 2:23-24

23 The man said, "This is now bone of my bones and flesh of my flesh; she shall be called 'woman,' for she was taken out of man."
24 That is why a man leaves his father and mother and is united to his wife, and they become one flesh.

Matthew 19:4-6

4 "Haven't you read," he replied, "that at the beginning the Creator 'made them male and female,' 5 and said, 'For this reason a man will leave his father and mother and be united to his wife, and the two will become one flesh'? 6 So they are no longer two, but one flesh. Therefore what God has joined together, let no one separate."

Mark 10:6-8

6 "But at the beginning of creation God 'made them male and female.' 7 'For this reason a man will leave his father and mother and be united to his wife, 8 and the two will become one flesh.' So they are no longer two, but one flesh.

Ephesians 5:30-31

30 for we are members of his body. 31 "For this reason a man will leave his father and mother and be united to his wife, and the two will become one flesh."

There are many areas in a marital relationship and it is these many areas that become "one" in the true believer's marriage. Working with many different couples over the years, I see that some of these areas in a marriage are:

1. Spiritual Beliefs,
2. Forgiveness,
3. Communication,
4. Conflict Resolution,
5. Financial Management,
6. Parenting,
7. Family & Friends,

We will discuss each of these briefly but understand that if we can get the first two on the list right, the remainder of the list is much easier. Believe me; I have seen it with my own eyes…more than once or twice.

Spiritual Beliefs

We discussed the importance of putting Christ first in our lives in chapter one. Therefore, we already know the importance of being "one" in our spiritual walk because it is most cardinal (i.e. important) and it drives the rest of our life. The spiritual oneness in a marriage cannot simply be to say that we are "believers", "Christians", "people of faith" etc. It has to be "walked out" in our daily lives. It is most important that we believe the whole Word of God and nothing but the Word of God. It is dangerous for even one person in the marriage or both to not believe everything that the Word of God tells us. When we carry any disbelief we are being double minded. James 1: 5-8 speaks to us about double mindedness and says:

*⁵ If any of you lacks wisdom, you should ask God, who gives generously to all without finding fault, and it will be given to you. ⁶ But when you ask, you must believe and not doubt, because the one who doubts is like a wave of the sea, blown and tossed by the wind. ⁷ That person should not expect to receive anything from the Lord. ⁸ Such a person is **double-minded** and unstable in <u>all</u> they do.*

Double mindedness is dangerous, first because it is not being obedient to the first and greatest commandment, and second it can lead to marital struggles due to a value *opposite* within the marriage. I recommend that we all find a true worship community, spend more time interacting with other true believers, reading and studying the true story that God has provided for us (The Holy Bible) and reading other literature that was influenced by the Word of God, like this one. These things will help us continue to understand the reality of God's Truth in our lives and in the culture we live in.

Forgiveness

Forgiveness is very important in a marriage and will more than likely have to be practiced daily. The lack of forgiveness destroys intimacy. Intimacy is not sex. Intimacy is closeness and friendship. It is deep, honest conversation and interaction. Intimacy means "I like you". Do you like your spouse? If you do not, it is probably because of some value opposite or there is some behavior that you have not forgiven. Jesus tells us that "*if you do not forgive others their sins, your Father will not forgive your sins* (Matthew 6:15). In Mark 11:25 it reads: "*[25] And when you stand praying, if you hold anything against anyone, forgive them, so that your Father in heaven may forgive you your sins.*" Luke 6:36-37 goes on to say "*[36] Be merciful, just as your Father is merciful.* [37] "..............*Forgive, and you will be forgiven.*" Therefore we can see the importance of forgiveness. It is important that when we think about forgiveness in our marriage. We do not only think about the "big things" that will need forgiveness, but we also think about the "little things". It is these little and big things, if gone unforgiven, that cause us not to have a true believer's' marriage and leads us to not "like" our spouse as a person, which leads to other struggles. It simply and horribly creates a snowball effect that decreases the occurrence of intimate moments in a marriage.

Do you love your spouse? Do you like your spouse? If you were to ask these questions to a married person, which one would be the hardest or take the longest to respond to? I always like to ask these two questions during sessions with couples. It is wonderful to hear that spouses not only confess to loving each other but also confess to liking each other. The amount of mutual respect, liking and friendship couples have for one another are important, especially after the first year of marriage.

Forgiveness will help with the development of this mutual intimacy.

Family & Friends

We have somewhat addressed this area previously in this chapter with some of the scriptures that was shared. Let's quickly look at this again. Jesus says in Matthew 19:4-6; *⁴"Haven't you read," he replied, "that at the beginning the Creator 'made them male and female,' ⁵ and said, 'For this reason a man will leave his father and mother and be united to his wife, and the two will become one flesh'? ⁶ So they are no longer two, but one flesh. Therefore what God has joined together, let no one separate."* Basically Jesus tells us that no man or woman should be allowed to come between you and your spouse. We are to separate from family and friends. This does not mean that we isolate from family and friends, just separate. However, even to "just separate" can be a difficult task for some. This separation can be an intimate and emotional separation. We all have different levels of intimacy with our family of origin and friends. This intimacy can range from enmeshment (i.e. overly involved) to being estranged (i.e. separated). Nevertheless, the "intimate" separation means that our family and friends do not make decisions in our lives or take up too much of our time. Decisions are discussed and made with our spouse. This can be complex but healthy boundaries have to be set in order for spouses to truly be "one". Boundary violations from family and friends will cause conflict in marriages.

A person operating from either end of the spectrum (enmeshed or estranged family and friend relationships) can hold on to the emotional implications of such relationships and carry them into the marriage. It is important to separate from the emotional implications of a negative family of origin and friend relationships. This will require forgiveness of family or friends' previous behaviors. Holding on to these negative emotions may interfere with you peacefully becoming one with your spouse. It is also important to separate from earlier romantic relationships or marriage partners as well as from the negative spirit of previous romantic relationships and marriage(s). These negative spirits are the conflicts that were part of the previous relationship that led or did not lead to the break up or divorce. We cannot treat our spouse like they have the same characteristics or expect our spouse to have the same characteristics of someone we previously dated or married…no matter what it is. I have seen someone in a marriage expect to have the same sexual interactions in their marriage that they once had in previous relationships and they would become frustrated when their spouse did not and could not do what their previous "lovers" did. We cannot bring the previous sin or conflicts from our past into our marriage and cause issues for our spouse in the marriage. These sins and conflicts can be related to passionate/sexual behaviors, intimacy or commitment. In order to build "oneness" there needs to be a healthy separation from our childhood family and others.

Communication and Conflict Resolution

I put these two areas together because conflict resolution often requires communication and communication can be conflictual. The three best suggestions I can give you pertaining to communication and conflict resolution is: 1) you are not in competition with your spouse, so do communicate with them like you are, 2) do not be selfish and egocentric when communicating and resolving conflicts in your marriage…try to see your spouse's perspective even if you have a different one and 3) be patient. As you can see, hopefully, these three suggestions are synonymous, parallel, and equivalent to "the two becoming one". Once the two have truly become one, communication and conflict resolution will look and feel different. Ephesians 5:28-31 helps us to understand this. It says:

[28] In this same way, husbands ought to love their wives as their own bodies. He who loves his wife loves himself. [29] After all, no one ever hated their own body, but they feed and care for their body, just as Christ does the church— [30] for we are members of his

body. [31] *"For this reason a man will leave his father and mother and be united to his wife, and the two will become one flesh."*

As we can see, one reason we become "one" in marriage is to be united in love towards one another. Therefore, there is no such thing as competition or "winning" in a true believer's marriage. You cannot win an argument. If your spouse feels defeated, then you both are defeated because you are "one".

Financial Management

Financial Management is another area that has to become "one" in a true believer's marriage. It has been said and supported through studies that financial problems are one of the biggest reasons for divorce. Is it really the financial problem that is the problem? Or is it is the couple having the financial problem that is the problem? I would argue for the latter. In our society finances (i.e. money) are very personal. More personal than most of us even realize. Many people, if not most, have some emotional connection to money. Also, the meaning given to money can be different from person to person. It is very important to understand how you and our spouse (or fiancé) view finances and how you both feel about money in different situations. First, it is very important to understand the first and greatest commandment that we discussed in chapter one. Matthew 6:24 says, *"No one can serve two masters. Either you will hate the one and love the other, or you will be devoted to the one and despise the other. You cannot serve both God and money."* It is obvious that God does not want us to put our finances before Him and there are different ways that this can happen. You should do an honest, honest, honest, appraisal of your life and how you handle your finances to see where you might put your finances before God. I used the word "honest" three times because I really want you to be honest.

Second, it is very important to understand that God calls us to be faithful overseers (i.e. stewards) of all He gives us as we can see in 1 Peter 4:10. It says, *"Each of you should use whatever gift you have received to serve others, as faithful stewards of God's grace in its various forms."* In this section of this book the form is finances. We definitely have to consider our tithing habits when we consider being good and faithful overseers of our finances. Giving to the body of Christ is a wonderful thing and I do not know anyone who tithes faithfully that does not reap what they have sown. However, some are skeptical about giving money to churches. Many churches do wonderful things with their resources and some do not, but tithing is definitely more than worth the effort to investigate and understand how different churches bless the community with their resources. Once you understand and have faith in how a church (or the one you attend) does that, you can faithfully tithe with the comfort of knowing that it is actually benefitting the body of Christ. I truly believe that "not tithing" (i.e. not contributing) to further the body of Christ is a mismanagement of finances and I have been there. We all know that the mismanagement of finances does not have positive consequences but managing our finances honestly is beneficial. There are many ways that we can mismanage our finances. Proverbs 13:11 says *"Dishonest money dwindles away, but whoever gathers money little by little makes it grow."* If you look close enough you will see that most people, who lie, cheat, steal or do something un-Godly to get their money are always "broke" or never satisfied. I have seen it many times and maybe you have as well. Therefore, understand that gathering your money honestly and sharing it responsibly is a blessing for the body of Christ and therefore the marriage of true believers.

We all have heard something about the "love of money". We have even confused having money with loving money. People that have money can love money and people who do not have money can also love money. No matter which group we find ourselves in, loving money is sinful, wicked, immoral and foul (i.e. evil). 1 Timothy 6:10 says, *"For the love of money is a root of all kinds of evil. Some people, eager for money, have wandered from the faith and pierced themselves with many griefs."* Loving money is dangerous and will cause you to be evil in your marriage and dating relationships. This may sound like strong language and you may believe that there is no way that you could be evil, but the Word of God says that the love of money is a root of all kinds of evil. That means more than one evil. It can tempt and cause you to lie, it can tempt and cause you to hide things, it can tempt and cause you to worry, it can tempt and cause your spouse to worry,...basically it can cause you to not be "one" with your spouse.

Some may disagree but I believe that married couples do not benefit from having separate bank accounts and paying "separate" bills, believers or not. There is no such thing as "separate" bills in a marriage. This situation breeds separateness that is opposite of "oneness". It is a symbolization of selfishness and/or mistrust in a holy covenant. It provides a greater opportunity for financial dishonesty. Always remember, "The two become one". Therefore, the finances before and after marriage and the debt before and after marriage become and remain "one". If combined accounts and combined bills have not worked for your marriage, seriously ask yourself why. Once you figure that out you will more than likely see changes that can be made to make it work. If you think combined accounts and combined bills will not work for your marriage, seriously ask yourself why. Once you figure that out you will more than likely see changes that can be made to make it work. It is simply my prayer that you can keep your lives free from the love of money and be content with what you have, because God has said, "Never will I leave you; never will I forsake you" (Hebrews 13:5).

Parenting

Having children is big responsibility but a bigger responsibility is maintaining a healthy marriage after children are born or adopted into the home and still the biggest responsibility is maintaining a healthy relationship with the Lord our God. Matthew 10: 37 says, *"Anyone who loves their father or mother more than me is not worthy of me; anyone who loves their son or daughter more than me is not worthy of me."* I start this section with this scripture because it reminds us of the first and greatest commandment and that is to love the Lord our God. Parent(s) can and do put the desires of their child before the desires of God in many situations. Parent(s) can and do compromise their values for their children, which is dangerous for the parent(s) and the child. It is very beneficial for children when the parents put the Lord our God first and the children are able to see the Lord work in their parents' lives. I have seen parents concerned and struggle with their child's behavior not being in line with the Christian faith too many times. And too many times I have heard these same parents say that they themselves have not been committed to the Christian faith. It really saddens me when I see and hear situations like this. It is like the parents expect their children to see the value in the Christian faith when their children do not have a parental example of the Christian faith at work. We can all learn from the wisdom given to us in Proverbs. Proverbs 22:6 says, *"Start children off on the way they should go, and even when they are old they will not turn from it."* We can see from this scripture that teaching and showing our children the importance of Christlikeness early in their lives is important. It actually insulates them from present and future sinful temptations, thoughts and behavior, which is good for their salvation. Proverbs 14:26 says, *"Whoever fears the Lord has a secure fortress, and for their children it will be a refuge."* Proverbs 20:7 says, *"The righteous lead blameless lives; blessed are their children after them."* We help our children to discover a wonderful and eternal refuge when we introduce and show them Christ and Christ-like behaviors and the righteous commandments of God. They need to see the Lord our God put first in our lives in order to take that inheritance into their adolescent and adult lives.

So, God is first, who is second? Well, the marriage of course! So where does that leave the children? Third? Basically, yes. We show our children that we truly love them when they are third on the list. I have shared with many couples that one of the best things they can give their child is an example of a successful Godly marriage. We want our children to learn to become "one" with their spouse once they decide to marry right? How can they learn that if they do not see their own parents becoming one with each other? I believe that there would be fewer divorces if parents could learn and practice not putting their children first and put them third. We are "one" with our spouse not our children. Our children grow up and move on, while we make a covenant to be with our spouse for a lifetime. Now let me say this…"the love we have for our spouse and the love we have for our children is different". It is apples and oranges. That is, spouses and children require different responses from us. It is a delicate dance and we have to be sure not to allow having children to severely decrease our marital "oneness" and satisfaction.

Now what about discipline? Well, that is delicate as well. What is discipline? It is self-control, self-restraint and correction. Proverbs 19:18 says, *"Discipline your children, for in that there is hope; do not be a willing party to their death."* There is little hope for children who are not disciplined. We truly take part in our children's destruction when we do not discipline them. Discipline teaches our children and discipline has to start very early. Proverbs 20:11 says, *"Even small children are known by their actions, so is their conduct really pure and upright?"* We have to consider the actions of even our small children and promote upright conduct in them. It is also important to consider the child as well as their actions. Every child needs discipline but the question is, "what kind of discipline?" Well, the answer is, "it depends on the child." Ephesians 6:4 says, *"Fathers, do not exasperate your children; instead, bring them up in the training and instruction of the Lord."* This simply means, do not madden, infuriate or enrage our children. I believe the Lord knows that when a person is maddened, infuriated or enraged, it is harder for them to effectively learn self-control, self-restraint and correction. So we have to learn what maddens, infuriates or enrages our children and not do that. There is a difference between being maddened, infuriated or enraged and having respectful fear. Each child is different and what works for one may infuriate the other. Some children may respond well to "spankings". Proverbs

13:24 says, *"Whoever spares the rod hates their children, but the one who loves their children is careful to discipline them."* From this scripture we can easily see that "spankings" can be effective and we also benefit from seeing that it is important to be careful to discipline our children. If the "rod" is effective and is needed in discipline, do not spare it. The trick is, discerning if it is effective and needed, because it may or may not be. The fact is, disciplining our children is a Godly thing and we can reap the benefits of it along with our children. Proverbs 29:17 says, *"Discipline your children, and they will give you peace; they will bring you the delights you desire."* They will also be prepared for the Lord, as Luke 1:17 says, *"And he will go on before the Lord, in the spirit and power of Elijah, to turn the hearts of the parents to their children and the disobedient to the wisdom of the righteous—to make ready a people prepared for the Lord."*

The truth of oneness is an excellent goal for confronting and mastering the inevitable crisis of life. Effective resolution of martial conflict requires a strategy, which seeks a solution that satisfies both spouses. Solutions offered by one spouse, no matter how correct they potentially may be, will not be effective if the other spouse does not agree with them. It is more beneficial to have cooperative efforts rather than hopeless compliance.

CHAPTER 3 - Digging Deeper

We are once again back to the part the chapter in which we will attempt to "dig deeper" by honestly considering specific questions related to what we just read in the chapter. Feel free to consider and discuss questions that you have that I did not include. I have provided another prayer to consider prior to addressing these questions. You can use the prayer that I have said and written below or you can say your own. The important thing is to pray.

Our Prayer for this chapter

Dear heavenly Father, our merciful and righteous Creator. Once again we come humbled and willing to know Your Truth for our marriage. We thank you for this opportunity to be with You as we explore our opposite characteristics. We pray that You give us the wisdom to understand what does and does not need to change in our marriage and the courage to make changes according to that wisdom. We pray that You help us to watch over the words that come out of our mouths as we discuss questions related to this chapter. In Jesus Christ's name we pray, AMEN!

Chapter 3 Questions
(Extra Space for Responses on pages 90-91)

1. What have been your thoughts about "oneness" in a marriage in the past?

2. What are your thoughts now about "oneness" now?

3. Can you think of any other areas of a marriage or dating relationship that I did not mention in the chapter?

4. Thinking about the areas of a relationship that I mentioned and other areas you can think of, in what areas of your marriage or dating relationship is "oneness" easiest or would be easiest? Why do you think this is?

5. Thinking about the areas of a relationship that I mentioned and other areas you can think of, in what areas of your marriage or dating relationship is "oneness" hardest or would be hardest? Why do you think this is?

6. In what areas could "oneness" improve in your marriage or dating relationship? What are some of your plans to improve these areas?

CHAPTER 4

The Dynamic Trio
Three is better than one or two?

There are three (3) components to a dating and martial relationship. Intimacy, commitment, and passion are the components. Every dating relationship and marriage has some degree of each component. Intimacy in a dating relationship or marriage is the degree of closeness and friendship shared by the man and woman. Commitment in a dating relationship or marriage is the degree of exclusivity between a man and woman. Passion in a dating relationship or marriage is the degree of emotion connected to being in the presence or thoughts of being in the presence of each other, which leads to romance. It is good for a marriage to have a healthy degree of each of these components. It is a blessing (and awesome) to have a high degree of each component that is based on genuine desire. That is, you and your spouse do things for each other ultimately because you want to do them. We want a marriage in which we do things out of love not exchange.

Some relationships have more problems than it has positive interactions and other relationships have more positive interactions than it has problems. Of course each of these situations has an effect on marriages and dating relationships. The social exchange marriage is an economic model of human behavior in which people are motivated by desire to maximize profit and minimize loss in their social relationships as if they are in business. Therefore the marriage or dating relationship is run like a business. There is sort of a "tit for tat" interaction. That is, we say "I will do something for you, if you do something for me" or "If you do not do something for me, I will not do something for you". In this type of relationship things are done out of reciprocation or obligation or things are withheld out of retaliation instead of out of love. Interacting with our spouses out of love sounds more like; "I do things for you simply because I love you, not because of what you have or have not done for me". The basic premise of social exchange marriage is simple: if the relationship provides more rewards and fewer costs there will be a more satisfying and enduring marriage. This is a "better to receive than to give" type of marriage. A true believer's marriage cannot be a social exchange marriage. There has to be far-reaching and wide-ranging love that includes healthy degrees of intimacy, commitment and passion.

Marriage Intimacy

Intimacy is a very important component in marriage. Healthy intimacy illustrates a rich friendship and closeness. It is when the married couple says that they are best friends and then acts like it in their daily interactions. When we see couples who look and act like best friends there is a high degree of intimacy. This is what God wants for us. We can see this in scripture that we find in Ephesians, Colossians, and I Peter. Ephesians 5:21-28 says:

21 Submit to one another out of reverence for Christ. 22 Wives, submit yourselves to your own husbands as you do to the Lord. 23 For the husband is the head of the wife as Christ is the head of the church, his body, of which he is the Savior. 24 Now as the church submits to Christ, so also wives should submit to their husbands in everything.
25 Husbands, love your wives, just as Christ loved the church and gave himself up for her 26 to make her holy, cleansing her by the washing with water through the word, 27 and to present her to himself as a radiant church, without stain or wrinkle or any other blemish, but holy and blameless. 28 In this same way, husbands ought to love their wives as their own bodies. He who loves his wife loves himself.

This scripture says a lot! It definitely speaks to intimacy. To submit means to yield and in order to be intimate with anyone we have to yield. Paul tells us in Colossians 3:18; *"Wives, submit yourselves to your husbands, as is fitting in the Lord"*. Many things could interfere with our desire to yield. Think about times when it is difficult for you to yield in any relationship. It is most difficult to yield when we do not like the person or something about the person, do not respect the person, "hold a grudge" against the person, or simply lack selflessness. Basically, unless it is lack of selflessness, we have not forgiven that person for some perceived trespass against us or someone else. This is why forgiveness is important. In a true believer's marriage intimacy can suffer if we do not practice daily forgiveness while maintaining a "marital peace treaty". A marital peace treaty means that we always seek peace in the marital relationship no matter what conflict may emerge, big or small. When we truly forgive, returning the marital relationship back to "peace" can be immediate, especially when dealing with small things (i.e. daily hassles). Seeking peace with bigger things can be immediate as well but definitely may take longer. The goal is to progress towards forgiveness and peace as soon as possible in order to prevent an interruption in yielding (i.e. submitting).

This scripture in Ephesians also tells us that *"the husband is the head of the wife as Christ is the head of the church"*. We have to truly understand Christ's relationship with His Church to understand what this means to marriage and intimacy. If you have not read the gospels with the purpose of understanding Christ's relationship with His Church, please do…right now. Christ loves the Church and gave his life for it. The Church is not only His bride but He also calls the Church His friend. In John 15:15 Jesus says *"I no longer call you servants, because a servant does not know his master's business. Instead, I have called you friends, for everything that I learned from my Father I have made known to you."* Christ is the head of the Church and therefore He is the head protector and servant of the

Church. He leads by example not just words. As "true believer husbands" we give our lives to our wives. We also act as the head protector and servant. That is, we lead our families in serving one another and in serving others. Giving our lives and serving our family are intimate behaviors. "Giving your life" can range from actually dying physically to giving up something for the sake of your wife's and your marriage. True believer husbands do not want to do anything that will tarnish his wife and therefore his marriage. Colossians 3:19 tells husbands to *"love your wives and do not be harsh with them"*. Maintaining persistent, Christ-like closeness and friendship is equivalent to love and giving.

Marriage Passion

Passion in a marriage is the degree of desire that you have for your spouse when you are in their presence or out of their presence, which leads to romance. Some might call it infatuation or having those "turned on" feelings. Romance typically includes sex in a marriage. However, it does not always include sex. In a true believer's marriage passion is sacred. That is, we have to oversee and make sure we keep the passionate part of our marriage holy. How do we do this? Well, one thing we do is attempt to understand what God expects from us. We can learn this from the Apostle Paul's letter to the church in Corinth. I Corinthians 7: 1-5 says:

¹ Now for the matters you wrote about: "It is good for a man not to have sexual relations with a woman." ² But since sexual immorality is occurring, each man should have sexual relations with his own wife, and each woman with her own husband. ³ The husband should fulfill his marital duty to his wife, and likewise the wife to her husband. ⁴ The wife does not have authority over her own body but yields it to her husband. In the same way, the husband does not have authority over his own body but yields it to his wife. ⁵ Do not deprive each other except perhaps by mutual consent and for a time, so that you may devote yourselves to prayer. Then come together again so that Satan will not tempt you because of your lack of self-control.

We learn a few things from this scripture. First, sex is only holy within a marriage and therefore if you are not married yet, you should refrain from having sex until you are married. If you have already started having sex, Stop! I know that it may be harder said than done but if you are planning on getting married you will be glad you stopped until the marriage. If you are not planning on getting married you will definitely be glad you stopped. Once you make the decision to stop, do not forget to repent and accept God's grace and mercy in your life and in your future marriage. Second, if you are married, passion becomes a collaborative and sometimes selfless interaction. The two becomes one flesh in passion. Therefore, in a true believer's marriage passion is shared when we are in the mood and even when we are not. That is not to say that we are to be inconsiderate of our spouse's moods. We are required to be loving and thankful to have a spouse who yields themselves for the sack of having passion and "oneness" in the marriage. This means that sometimes there will be sex and sometimes there will not, which takes us to the third thing. Third, we are not to be inconsiderate or vindictive with our passion. We cannot use the lack of sex as a weapon or a punishment. This violates the lack of authority we have over our own bodies once we marry. We can also easily become preoccupied with life and create interference in our sex lives. We must be aware when this is happening. The only thing that God sees as an appropriate interference in our martial sex lives is prayer. Therefore, the time we devote to Him should be the only thing that trumps passion in our marriages. Fourth, sex is a component in marriage to help us have self-control. There is more self-control when passionate desires are met within the marriage. The lack of sex in a marriage can cause a spouse to be tempted outside of the marriage, which is very dangerous. We all know what that danger is, without saying, but I will say it anyway...Adultery. In my years working with couples, I have also found that the death of intimacy (closeness and friendship) in a marriage can also lead to adultery. Some of us cannot imagine ourselves or our spouse committing adultery. Some of us just cannot vision that. Well, we have to make sure that we understand what Jesus says about adultery to make sure we pray not to be led into temptation, but to be delivered from that evil. Jesus says in Matthew 5:27-28:

27 "You have heard that it was said, 'You shall not commit adultery.' 28 But I tell you that anyone who looks at a woman lustfully has already committed adultery with her in his heart.

Wow! Now that broadens the possibilities for being tempted to commit adultery. We could commit adultery at the grocery store, we could commit adultery at church, we could commit adultery at the mall, we could commit adultery while watching television, and we could commit adultery on our computers and other electronic devices. This is just to name a few. In a true believer's marriage we cannot even introduce pornography to our marriage because that would be adultery. I mention that because I have worked with couples who were using pornography for some reason or another. I do not remember one couple who did not eventually have a problem in their marriage when pornography was used. The bottom line is that we know sexual behavior is sacred and preserved for marriage between a man and woman. Proverbs 6:32-33 says:

32 But a man who commits adultery has no sense; whoever does so destroys himself. 33 Blows and disgrace are his lot, and his shame will never be wiped away.

Hebrews 13:3-5 says:

4 Marriage should be honored by all, and the marriage bed kept pure, for God will judge the adulterer and all the sexually immoral.

Recovering from any form of adultery is difficult due the betrayal nature of adultery and the potential shame that accompanies adultery. However, I have definitely seen couples overcome that evil. One specific goal is to have open communication about desires for passion. The general goal is to become "one" in passion.

Marriage Commitment

Commitment in a dating relationship or marriage is the degree of exclusivity between a man and woman. That is, "there is no one else like you in my life". Some would say that a marital relationship with no commitment is no marriage at all. The marriage vows that we say at marital ceremonies are centered on commitment. It typically goes like this "I,____, take thee,_____, to be my lawful wedded Wife/Husband, to have and to hold from this day forward, for better for worse, for richer for poorer, in sickness and in health, to love and to cherish, till death us do part, according to God's holy ordinance; and thereto I plight thee my troth" or it may go like this "I, ____, take you, ____, to be my lawfully wedded(husband/wife), to have and to hold, from this day forward, for better, for worse, for richer, for poorer, in sickness and in health, until death do us part." We are vowing to be committed to our spouse. Our Lord and Savior Jesus Christ explains marital commitment to us in the book of Matthew. Matthew 19: 3-10 says:

3 Some Pharisees came to him to test him. They asked, "Is it lawful for a man to divorce his wife for any and every reason?"
4 "Haven't you read," he replied, "that at the beginning the Creator 'made them male and female,' 5 and said, 'For this reason a man will leave his father and mother and be united to his wife, and the two will become one flesh'? 6 So they are no longer two, but one flesh. Therefore what God has joined together, let no one separate."
7 "Why then," they asked, "did Moses command that a man give his wife a certificate of divorce and send her away?"
8 Jesus replied, "Moses permitted you to divorce your wives because your hearts were hard. But it was not this way from the beginning. 9 I tell you that anyone who divorces his wife, except for sexual immorality, and marries another woman commits adultery."
10 The disciples said to him, "If this is the situation between a husband and wife, it is better not to marry."

We see here that divorce is only accepted if there has been sexual immorality within the marriage. I found it a little funny that when the disciples heard this mandate given by Jesus for divorce, they stated that it is better not to marry. It is as if they thought marriage would be too difficult if adultery was the only reason they could get a divorce. Paul speaks about commitment as well. We find this scripture in I Corinthians. I Corinthians 7: 12-16 says:

12 To the rest I say this (I, not the Lord): If any brother has a wife who is not a believer and she is willing to live with him, he must not divorce her. 13 And if a woman has a husband who is not a believer and he is willing to live with her, she must not divorce him. 14 For the unbelieving husband has been sanctified through his wife, and the unbelieving wife has been sanctified through her believing husband. Otherwise your children would be unclean, but as it is, they are holy.

15 But if the unbeliever leaves, let it be so. The brother or the sister is not bound in such circumstances; God has called us to live in peace. 16 How do you know, wife, whether you will save your husband? Or, how do you know, husband, whether you will save your wife?

Peter speaks about commitment in 1 Peter. 1 Peter 3:1-2, 7 says:

Wives, in the same way submit yourselves to your own husbands so that, if any of them do not believe the word, they may be won over without words by the behavior of their wives, 2 when they see the purity and reverence of your lives.

7 Husbands, in the same way be considerate as you live with your wives, and treat them with respect as the weaker partner and as heirs with you of the gracious gift of life, so that nothing will hinder your prayers.

This issue (i.e. headache) that Paul and Peter speak of would seem not to be an issue if we are careful to make sure that we are equally yoked with someone before we say "I do". Nevertheless, this issue they speak of is not sexual immorality and therefore the marital commitment stands. In 1 Corinthians 7:39 Paul goes on to say:

39 A woman is bound to her husband as long as he lives. But if her husband dies, she is free to marry anyone she wishes, but he must belong to the Lord.

Here Paul expresses the "until death do us part" phrase that we see in our wedding vows today. He also advises us to marry someone who is led by the Lord if we remarry. This will keep us from dealing what Paul spoke about in 1 Corinthians 7:12-16 and what Peter spoke about in 1 Peter 3:1-2.

CHAPTER 4 - Digging Deeper

We are once again back to the part the chapter in which we will attempt to "dig deeper" by honestly considering specific questions related to what we just read in the chapter. Feel free to consider and discuss questions that you have that I did not include. I have provided another prayer to consider prior to addressing these questions. You can use the prayer that I have said and written below or you can say your own. As always the important thing is to pray.

Our Prayer for this chapter

Dear heavenly Father, the great I AM. Once again we come exalting you, wanting to know Your Truth for our marriage. We thank you for this opportunity to be in Your presence as we explore the intimacy, passion and commitment in our marriage. We pray that You give us divine wisdom to understand what does and does not need to change in our marriage and the courage to make changes according that wisdom. We pray that You help us to watch over the words that come out of our mouths as we discuss questions related to this chapter. In Jesus Christ's name we pray, AMEN!

Chapter 4 Questions
(Extra Space for Responses on pages 92-93)

1. Do you think or feel that you have some aspects of a social exchange relationship in your marriage or dating relationship?

2. Discuss the feelings, thoughts, and behaviors you have had when you felt your spouse had neglected some aspect of your relationship. Discuss the feelings, thoughts, and behaviors you would have if you felt your spouse had neglected some aspect of your relationship. Would you feel the urge to stop doing something for them?

3. What would you say about the friendship and closeness in your marriage?

4. How could you enhance and enrich the friendship and closeness in your marriage?

5. What would say about the passion in your marriage?

6. How could you enhance and enrich the passion in your marriage?

7. What would you say about the commitment in your marriage?

8. How could you enhance and enrich the commitment in your marriage?

CHAPTER 5

Things to do
Where Your Faith Meets Works

First Thing First

I hope you have faith in your marriage or dating relationship at this point. If not and you are married, pray for your spouse, pray with your spouse, pray for your marriage, find scripture that illustrates the awesomeness of our God and go back and read chapter one. The truth is, if we can increase our faith in God, all else becomes much easier. Philippians 4:12-13 says:

[12] I know what it is to be in need, and I know what it is to have plenty. I have learned the secret of being content in any and every situation, whether well fed or hungry, whether living in plenty or in want. [13] I can do all this through him who gives me strength.

Isaiah 54: 17 says:

[17] no weapon forged against you will prevail, and you will refute every tongue that accuses you. This is the heritage of the servants of the Lord, and this is their vindication from me," declares the Lord.

When it is all said and done we want to be able to say what Paul said in 2 Timothy. 2 Timothy 4:7 says:

7 I have fought the good fight, I have finished the race, I have kept the faith.

Other Things Second

Next, I want to give you a few resources that you will hopefully be some of your "works" that is driven by the faith you have in God and your marriage. These are basically exercises that will hopefully help to enhance and enrich your marriage. The first thing I want you to do is a *Marriage Mission Statement*. This is a statement of what you want your marriage to be. This will allow you to develop a foundational document that will drive your marriage and give you something to refer to periodically throughout your marriage. Some couples go as far as framing their *Marriage Mission Statement* and hanging it somewhere special in their home. See below and complete. Be sure to complete the individual marriage mission statements first. Complete these without the help or input of your spouse. Then come together as a couple and complete the unified marriage mission statement. (*Complete Mission Statements of Pages 95-97*)

Our Marriage Mission Statement

His:

Hers:

Unified:

Husband (print): _____

Wife (print): _____

Sign: _____

Sign: _____

Date: _____

The second thing I want you to do is what I call *Stimulus - Value – Role assessment.* This will allow you to explore what attracted you to your spouse, the "oneness" of your values, and the roles that you have in the relationship. See below, put your spouse's name in the blanks, and respond to the five questions. Use another sheet of paper to write down your responses, if needed. Be sure to share your responses with each other.

Stimulus-Value-Role

How did you perceive _____
external attributes, physical appearance, and behavior when you <u>first</u> met them or <u>first</u> decided that they were favorable or desirable?

As you "got to know" _____
what values and attitudes did you perceive to be compatible to your values and attitudes?

As you "got to know" _____
what values and attitudes did you perceive to not be compatible to your values and attitudes?

What are your current roles in your relationship with _____?

What roles do you not have that you think you should have in your relationship with
_____?

The third thing I want you to do is the 5 Love Languages assessment. You may have done this before as it is a poplar resource. I recommend that you purchase the book called *The 5 Love Languages: The Secret to Love That Last* by Gary Chapman as this book will give you a greater understanding on how to best respond to your spouse's love language. I believe it is important to know that Gary Chapman is Christian author. The objective of this exercise is to improve the love in your relationship. Therefore, once you discover your spouse's love language, be sure to start doing things that coincide with their love language. It is simply more fruitful.

The 5 Love Languages®

What if you could say or do just the right thing guaranteed to make that special someone feel loved? The secret is learning the right love language! Millions of couples have learned the simple way to express their feelings and bring joy back into marriage by using, "The 5 Love Languages", by Dr. Gary Chapman (New York Times bestseller) as a resource. The 5 love languages are as follows:

#1: Words of Affirmation
Actions don't always speak louder than words. If this is your love language, unsolicited compliments mean the world to you. Hearing the words, "I love you," are important—hearing the reasons behind that love sends your spirits skyward. Insults can leave you shattered and are not easily forgotten.

#2: Quality Time

For those whose love language is spoken with Quality Time, nothing says, "I love you," like full, undivided attention. Being there for this type of person is critical, but really being there—with the TV off, fork and knife down, and all chores and tasks on standby—makes your significant other feel truly special and loved. Distractions, postponed dates, or the failure to listen can be especially hurtful.

#3: Receiving Gifts

Don't mistake this love language for materialism; the receiver of gifts thrives on the love, thoughtfulness, and effort behind the gift. If you speak this language, the perfect gift or gesture shows that you are known, you are cared for, and you are prized above whatever was sacrificed to bring the gift to you. A missed birthday, anniversary, or a hasty, thoughtless gift would be disastrous—so would the absence of everyday gestures.

#4: Acts of Service

Can vacuuming the floors really be an expression of love? Absolutely! Anything you do to ease the burden of responsibilities weighing on an "Acts of Service" person will speak volumes. The words he or she most want to hear: "Let me do that for you." Laziness, broken commitments, and making more work for them tell speakers of this language their feelings don't matter.

#5: Physical Touch

This language isn't all about the bedroom. A person whose primary language is Physical Touch is, not surprisingly, very touchy. Hugs, pats on the back, holding hands, and thoughtful touches on the arm, shoulder, or face—they can all be ways to show excitement, concern, care, and love. Physical presence and accessibility are crucial, while neglect or abuse can be unforgivable and destructive.

Now! Take a guess what your spouse's or spouse to be Love Language is and have them to guess yours.

☐ A = Words of Affirmation
☐ B = Quality Time
☐ C = Receiving Gifts
☐ D = Acts of Service
☐ E = Physical Touch

Now to be sure, go online to take the actual quiz at www.5lovelanguages.com/assessment. Dr. Gary Chapman's book, *The Five Love Languages,* can be purchased at your local bookstore, or through www.amazon.com. Be sure to start putting your knowledge of your spouse's love language into action. That is the only purpose of this exercise. Now you know and therefore there is no excuse. I am so happy for you and your spouse.

Personal Style

The fourth thing that I recommend is the *Interpersonal Style Assessment*. This resource helps with communication, intimacy, and conflict resolution. The Interpersonal Style Assessment will give you information on how your spouse and you assert yourselves and how your spouse and you orient yourselves. It will tell you if you are "tell assertive" or "ask assertive". It will tell you if you are "task oriented" or "people oriented". It will also tell you how your spouse and you initially respond to conflict and the progression of that conflict response if the conflict is not resolved. I have provided the two Interpersonal Styles Assessments that I use with couples. However, unless you have made an appointment with me, you are sort of left on your own as it relates to understanding, predicting and responding to yours and your spouse's interpersonal style but I will do my best to walk you through it all in this chapter. The goal is to increase your interpersonal intelligence. Two things happen when you do this: 1) You gain recognition of your personal strengths and weaknesses and ability to use that information about yourself to respond appropriately to your spouse and 2) you gain the ability to detect and respond appropriately to the mood, temperaments, motives and intentions of your spouse. Complete the two Interpersonal Style Assessments by following the instructions of each one.

INTERPERSONAL STYLE QUESTIONNAIRE

Put a check mark by each statement that you believe
is a fair representation of
(spouse's name) _____.

Analytical	Driver
☐ Gives priority to detail and organization ☐ Sets exacting standards ☐ Approaches tasks and people with steadiness ☐ Enjoys research and analysis ☐ Prefers operating within guidelines ☐ Completes tasks thoroughly ☐ Focuses attention on immediate task ☐ Likes accuracy ☐ Makes decisions on thorough basis ☐ Values standard procedures highly ☐ Approaches work systematically ☐ Likes to plan for change ☐ Likes to think before they act TOTAL : _____	☐ Gives priority to achieving results ☐ Seeks challenges ☐ Approaches tasks and people with clear goals ☐ Is willing to confront ☐ Makes decisions easily ☐ Is keen to progress ☐ Feels a sense of urgency ☐ Acts with authority ☐ Likes to take the lead ☐ Enjoys solving problems ☐ Questions the status quo ☐ Takes action to bring about change ☐ Likes to be in control TOTAL : _____

Amiable	Expressive
☐ Gives priority to supporting others ☐ Enjoys assisting others ☐ Approaches people and tasks with quiet and caution ☐ Has difficulty saying no ☐ Values co-operation over competition ☐ Eager to get on with others ☐ Willing to show loyalty ☐ Calms excited people ☐ Listens well/attentively ☐ Prefers others to take the lead ☐ Gives priority to secure relationships & situations ☐ Prefers steady not sudden change ☐ Peacemaker TOTAL : _____	☐ Gives priority to creating a friendly environment ☐ Likes an informal style ☐ Approaches people and tasks with energy ☐ Emphasizes enjoying oneself ☐ Rates creativity highly ☐ Prefers broad approach to details ☐ Likes participating in groups ☐ Creates a motivational environment ☐ Acts on impulse ☐ Willing to express feelings ☐ Enjoys discussing possibilities ☐ Keen to promote change ☐ Values the opinion of others TOTAL : _____

Note: The quadrant with the most check marks indicates Interpersonal Style.

INTERPERSONAL STYLES ASSESSMENT

Completed By: _____

Instructions: To determine your spouse's Interpersonal Styles, circle the number or letter in each of the scales below that best represent how you perceive your spouse.

I Would Best Describe_____ **As:**

goes along............take charge	private......................warm
D C B A	1 2 3 4
quiet...........................talkative	calm.....................excitable
D C B A	1 2 3 4
supportive..............challenging	task-oriented...people-oriented
D C B A	1 2 3 4
compliant..................dominant	eyes serious............eyes friendly
D C B A	1 2 3 4
ask questions....makes statements	talks only..........shares personal business feelings
D C B A	1 2 3 4
cooperative..............competitive	reserved....................outgoing
D C B A	1 2 3 4
introverted..............extroverted	wants or uses........wants or uses facts opinions
D C B A	1 2 3 4
slow, studied.................fast paced	does not express.......expresses emotion emotions
D C B A	1 2 3 4
constrained........................open	objectives.................personal
D C B A	1 2 3 4

Totals: Total the number of times that each letter and number is circled.

D__   C__   B__   A__

1__   2__   3__   4__

The letter and number with the highest totals combine to represent an approximation of Interpersonal Styles by verbal and nonverbal behavior. Use the Interpersonal Style Matrix to show where your highest letter and number intersect. This will show your approximate style.

Interpersonal Styles Matrix

Instructions
Determine your spouse's approximate Interpersonal Style by using the matrix below.

	D	**C**	**B**	**A**
1 **2**	**Analytical** (Ask Assertive and Task Oriented)		**Driver** (Tell Assertive and Task Oriented)	
3 **4**	**Amiable** (Ask Assertive and People Oriented)		**Expressive** (Tell Assertive and People Oriented)	

The 4 Interpersonal Styles

Here are descriptions of the four interpersonal styles:

Analytical Style people value facts above all, and may appear uncommunicative, cool and independent. They have a strong time discipline coupled with a slow pace to action. They value accuracy, competency and logic over opinions, often avoiding risk in favor of cautious, deliberate decisions. Analyticals are usually cooperative, providing they have some freedom to organize their own efforts. In relationships, Analyticals are initially more careful and reserved, but once trust is earned they can become dedicated and loyal.

Amiable Style people are people-oriented, and care more about close relationships than results or influence. They usually appear warm, friendly and cooperative. Amiables tend to move slowly with a low time discipline, minimizing risk and often using personal opinions to arrive at decisions. Belonging to a group is a primary need, and Amiables may make every effort to gain acceptance. They typically seek to uncover common ground, preferring to achieve objectives through understanding and mutual respect rather than force and authority. When influence with force, Amiables may appear to cooperate initially but will likely lack commitment to whatever the feel forced to do and may later resist implementation or interaction.

Expressive Style people are motivated by recognition, approval and prestige. They tend to appear communicative and approachable, often sharing their feelings and thoughts. They move quickly, continually excited about the next big idea, but they often don't commit to specific plans or see things through to completion. Expressives enjoy taking risks. When making decisions, they tend to place more stock in the opinions of prominent or successful people than in logic or research. Though they consider relationships important, the Expressive's competitive nature leads them to seek quieter friends who are supportive of their dreams and ideas, often making relationships shallow or short-lived.

Driving Style people want to know the estimated outcome of each option. They are willing to accept risks, but want to move quickly and have the final say. In relationships, they may appear uncommunicative, independent and competitive. Driving styles tend to focus on efficiency or productivity rather than devoting time and attention to casual relationships. They seldom see a need to share personal motives or feelings. Driving styles are results-oriented, tending to initiate action and give clear direction. They seek control over their environment.

Response to Conflict (4 step process for each style)

Here you will see the "4 step" process each interpersonal style. When there is conflict the *analytical* may have a response pattern like this:

Analytical Style (Avoiding)
1st Response = Avoids Confrontation, Draws attention away from issue, Delays Decisions

2nd Response = Confronts others (Autocratic), Focuses on the issue, Becomes demanding

3rd Response = Smoothes relationships, Yields to others views, Waivers on opinion, hesitates

4th Response = Confronts others, Verbalizes judgmental feelings, Blames others personally

When there is conflict the *amiable* may have a response pattern like this:

Amiable (Peace-maker, Acquiescing)
1st Response = Smoothes relationships, Yields to others views, Waivers on opinion, hesitates

2nd Response = Confronts others, Verbalizes judgmental feelings, Blames others personally

3rd Response = Avoids Confrontation, Draws attention away from issue, Delays Decisions

4th Response = Confronts others (Autocratic), Focuses on the issue, Becomes demanding

When there is conflict the *expressive* may have a response pattern like this:

Expressive (Attacking)
1st Response = Confronts others, Verbalizes judgmental feelings, Blames others personally

2nd Response = Smoothes relationships, Yields to others views, Waivers on opinion, hesitates

3rd Response = Confronts others (Autocratic), Focuses on the issue, Becomes demanding

4th Response = Avoids Confrontation, Draws attention away from issue, Delays Decisions

When there is conflict the *driver* may have a response pattern like this:

Driver (Autocratic)
1st Response = Confronts others (Autocratic), Focuses on the issue, Becomes demanding

2nd Response = Avoids Confrontation, Draws attention away from issue, Delays Decisions

3rd Response = Confronts others, Verbalizes judgmental feelings, Blames others personally

4th Response = Smoothes relationships, Yields to others views, Waivers on opinion, hesitates

The goal is to understand how you and your spouse typically respond to conflict in order for you both to decide when that response is appropriate or not. Does our response promote the "oneness" that God wants us to have in our marriage? Sometimes it may and sometimes it may not. We have to be aware of when it does not promote that "oneness" and change our response to resolve the conflict in a timely manner. For example, if an analytical, who is married to an expressive, wants to delay they have to understand if this is a good time to delay because the expressive will probably not want to delay and not delaying may be best. Likewise the expressive has to look at the situation and decide if delaying would be better even though they do not wish to delay. You as a married couple have to be aware of your different interactions and seek "oneness". What typically happens is you and your spouse progress from one response to the next when a response is not resolving the conflict. It is not good for your spouse or you to get all the way to their 4th response because this is a last resort for them and usually is a very uncomfortable response for them because it is furthest from their initial response.

Prepare and Enrich

The fifth thing that I recommend is the PREPARE/ENRICH Assessment. This was also developed by Christian counselors. I recommend that you find a local counselor who administers and interprets this assessment and make an appointment with them. You can do this by going to www.prepare-enrich.com. Once you are at the website, go to "For Couples" and you will see "find a facilitator" at the bottom of the page. You will also see other resources related to PREPARE/ENRICH of which you can take advantage.

CHAPTER 5 - Digging Deeper

We are once again back to the part the chapter in which we will attempt to "dig deeper" by honestly considering specific questions related to what we just read in the chapter. Feel free to consider and discuss questions that you have that I did not include. I have provided another prayer to consider prior to addressing these questions. You can use the prayer that I have said and written below or you can say your own. As always the important thing is to pray.

Our Prayer for this chapter

Dear heavenly Father, we thank you for this time that we have together with you in order to seek a true believer's marriage. We thank you for the days and experiences that we have had with each other. We thank you for the opportunity to seek Holiness in our marriages. Be with us as we continue to understand our relationship so that our marriage will honor you. We pray that You help us to watch over the words that come out of our mouths as we discuss questions related to this chapter. In Jesus Christ's name we pray, AMEN!

Chapter 5 Questions
(*Extra Space for Responses on page 94*)
1. How did you experience completing the assessments in this chapter?

2. Which assessment do you think will be most beneficial for your marriage in seeking a true believer's marriage?

3. Having s true believer's marriage is an ongoing adventure. How do you plan to make sure that you stay on track during this adventure?

CHAPTER ONE RESPONSES

1.

2.

3.

4.

CHAPTER ONE RESPONSES

5.

6.

7.

CHAPTER TWO RESPONSES

1.

2.

3.

4.

CHAPTER TWO RESPONSES

5.

CHAPTER THREE RESPONSES

1.

2.

3.

4.

CHAPTER THREE RESPONSES

5.

6.

CHAPTER FOUR RESPONSES

1.

2.

3.

4.

CHAPTER FOUR RESPONSES

5.

6.

7.

8.

CHAPTER FIVE RESPONSES

1.

2.

3.

HIS MARRIAGE MISSION STATEMENT

HER MARRIAGE MISSION STATEMENT

UNIFIED MARRIAGE MISSION STATEMENT

REFLECTIONS
Reflect on What You Have Learned

NOTES

NOTES

Made in the USA
Monee, IL
10 August 2021

75335798R00059